WHAT A BLAST!

By Julie Winterbottom

Illustrations by Clau Souza

T0371867

Workman Publishing
New York

*This book is dedicated to our hardworking digestive bacteria,
without which our lives would be tragically fart-free.*

Acknowledgments

*The author would like to thank the following people for their help with this book:
Pam Bobowicz, Jim Chapin, Chris Duffy, Gracie Elliott, Sue Macy,
and, bringing up the rear end, Stephen Wetta.*

Library of Congress Cataloging-in-Publication Data

Title: What a blast! : fart games, fart puzzles, fart pranks, and more farts! / by Julie Winterbottom;
illustrated by Claudia Souza. Description: New York : Workman Publishing Co., Inc., [2022] Identifiers:
LCCN 2021042934 | ISBN 9781523513499 (paperback) Subjects: LCSH: Flatulence—Juvenile literature.
Classification: LCC RC862.F55 W56 2022 | DDC 616.3002/07
—dc23 LC record available at https://lccn.loc.gov/2021042934

The author and publisher disclaim responsibility for any adverse effects that result
from using information contained in this book.

Design by John Passineau
Cover illustration by Clau Souza

Workman books are available at special discounts when purchased in bulk for premiums and sales promotions as well
as for fundraising or educational use. Special editions or book excerpts can also be created to specification.
For details, contact the Special Sales Director at specialmarkets@workman.com.

Workman Publishing Co., Inc.
225 Varick Street
New York, NY 10014-4381
workman.com

Printed in China on responsibly sourced paper
First printing May 2022

10 9 8 7 6 5 4 3 2 1

PFFFFFFT!!!!

Ooh, someone just farted.

Was that you? Yes? Excellent! You've come to the right place. This book is for people who appreciate that there is nothing funnier than a blast of wind erupting from someone's butt.

What is it exactly that makes farts so funny, anyway? It probably has to do with the fact that we really can't control them. *Pffffftt.* (See? Was that you again?) Farts pop out without our permission and remind the world that no matter who we are or what we do, we all have gassy things going on inside our bodies that come out our back ends.

In this book you get to celebrate farts in all their hilarious, stinking, honking glory. The pages are bloated with farty quizzes, jokes, stories, puzzles, and pranks. There are even pages for you to fart on. (Yes, you read that correctly. You can fart *in* this book.) And there are tons of fart facts. There's a lot to learn about farting because all people and most animals do it. You'll be a walking, farting encyclopedia of stink.

Pfftttt. Speaking of which, did you fart *again*? Wow, you just can't stop! We'd better get going before you run out of gas.

PFFFFFFT!!!!

PFFT!

Part 1: Your Life as a Farter

You cut your first fart the day you were born, and you won't stop breaking wind until the day you die (actually, a little after that). Farting is one of the weirdest, silliest, most obnoxious things your body does. There *is* a reason for it, though, and we'll get to the bottom of it. Get ready to celebrate your most outstanding productions and give the gift of gas to the ones you love.

What do you call
a toxic fart quietly dropped
by someone's father?

Silent
but *dadly.*

The Science Behind Your Behind

Why exactly do we fart? A quick trip through your body's hardworking digestive system reveals the answer. The journey begins when you pop some food into your mouth.

1 Chewing breaks the food into smaller pieces, and your saliva moistens it so you can swallow it.

2 The soggy ball of food travels along a tube called the *esophagus.*

3 At the end of the tube is your stomach. There the food mixes with powerful acids and digestive enzymes to create a thick, liquidy goop called *chyme.*

4 The next stop is the all-important small intestine. Here, more enzymes break down the nutrients in the chyme and those nutrients get absorbed into your bloodstream. Stuff that can't be digested by the enzymes travels on.

5 In the large intestine, tiny organisms called *bacteria* break down the undigested parts of the food so they can exit your body as poop. As they work, the bacteria produce gas.

6 *PFFT!* The gas leaves by the nearest exit—the *anus,* otherwise known as the hole in your bottom.

What did **one** burp say to the other burp?

Let's go out the other end!

Are You a Frequent Farter?

The average person farts 10 to 20 times a day. What's your toot tally? Keep track of every fart you emit for three days straight, from when you wake up until you go to sleep. Don't forget to include the silent ones! You can have a friend do the same thing and then compare your totals here to see who is fartier.

The Smelly Truth A whopping 99 percent of farts are completely odorless. Farts that stink have small amounts of sulfur, which smells like rotten eggs. If you want to add some powerful perfume to your wind, eat foods that contain sulfur, such as eggs, red meat, and cauliflower.

My Fart Total

Day 1 _____

Day 2 _____

Day 3 _____

Observations

_____

_____

_____

_____

My Friend's Fart Total

Day 1 _____

Day 2 _____

Day 3 _____

Observations

_____

_____

_____

_____

What Do You Think About the Stink?

Some people are bold and unapologetic about cutting the cheese. Others think gut gas is so gross it should be outlawed. What's your attitude about farting? Take this quiz to find out. Circle one answer for each question. Then add up your points at the end to find your farting identity.

1 You are hanging out with friends and are about to fart. What do you do?

A. Leave, immediately. You'd rather die than let anyone hear you fart.

B. Try to hold it in and pray it won't be a stinker if it comes out.

C. Relax, knowing that your fart will crack everyone up.

D. Interrupt the conversation, lift your butt cheek, and say, "Listen to this!"

2 Someone farts during math class. What do you do?

A. Glare at them like they just released poison into the air and move your chair away.

B. Pretend nothing happened.

C. Try not to giggle.

D. Let one rip in return.

3 Your friend's dog lets out a fart that's breathtakingly awful. What do you do?

A. You scream, open all the windows, and suggest the dog stay outside from now on.

B. You think how glad you are it was him and not you.

C. You shriek with laughter at how horrible the smell is.

D. You look at the dog with envy and say, "Wow. How did you *do* that?"

4 **Have you ever recorded one of your own farts?**

A. Are you crazy? That's disgusting!

B. No, it's embarrassing enough to fart once. I don't want a record of it.

C. No, but it's a funny idea!

D. Of course. Hasn't everyone?

5 **Your preferred place to fart is:**

A. Not anyone's business.

B. Anywhere you can be alone.

C. In school, where you can make everyone laugh.

D. On stage, in the library, while taking a test—anyplace and anytime people will be sure to hear it.

6 **You're at a movie theater waiting for the film to begin when you let slip a silent but deadly fart. What do you do?**

A. Act like it was someone else. Look around, sniff, and say, "Ew, what *is* that?"

B. Stare at your phone and hope no one can see how badly you are blushing.

C. Say something funny, like, "Um, does anyone have a gas mask I can borrow?"

D. Smile proudly and say, "Now *that's* Oscar-worthy!"

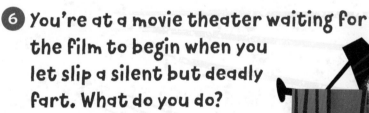

ADD UP YOUR POINTS. GIVE YOURSELF:

1 point for every **A**: _____

2 points for every **B**: _____

3 points for every **C**: _____

4 points for every **D**: _____

TOTAL: _____

Now turn the page to find out what your fartitude is.

YOUR FARTITUDE

Add up your points for the quiz on pages 6-7. Then find your fart personality here.

6-10 points: Disgusted Denier

You think farting is so gross that you won't even admit you do it. And you flee when others do.

11-16 points: Shy, Controlled Farter

You feel mortified when you or someone else breaks wind, and you try desperately to hold it when you're in public.

17–20 points: Joyful, Comedic Farter

You think farts are hilarious, whether they are your own or someone else's, and you never hesitate to enjoy the show.

21–24 points: Proud, Competitive Farter

You let it rip shamelessly, no matter where you are or whose nose you offend. You have never in your life suppressed a fart and have been known to force the issue when you feel one emerging.

The Smelly Truth On average, people produce enough gas each day to fill two soda cans. Yum!

What Kind of Farter Are You?

Now that you've figured out your general attitude about butt bursts, get to know your farty self even better here.

I am a _____ farter.

When I fart, it makes me feel _____ .

My favorite time to fart is _____ .

The most embarassing time I ever farted was _____ .

The people I most like to fart with are _____ .

The most talented farter I know is _____ .

One way I could increase my fart-bravery is to _____ .

If I could fart anywhere in the world, I would choose _____ .

My favorite kind of fart is _____ ,

but someday I'd like to try _____ .

The Smelly Truth According to a study, men fart more often than women, but women's farts are more likely to stink because they contain more sulfur.

Free the Fart!

Help this fart travel through the extra-long maze of intestines and find its way into the world!

The answer is on page 103.

The Smelly Truth Farts and burps both carry gas out of your body. The main difference (besides the end they come out of) is that burps release air that gets into your stomach when you swallow, while farts release gas from your large intestine.

Fart for a Cause

Test your trickster skills and your fart power with this prank pledge form.

WHAT TO DO: Cut out the Fart-a-Thon pledge form below. Then show it to your parents, friends, relatives, neighbors—anyone with a sense of humor—and ask them to sponsor you. If they fall for it, you might end up farting in a park for 30 minutes!

Show Your Spirit!

PLEDGE FORM

I am participating in a new fundraising event called a "Fart-a-Thon" to raise money for

_____.
                          CAUSE

A Fart-a-Thon is just like a Walk-a-Thon, only participants raise money by farting instead of walking!

The event will take place on _____ at _____.
                                    DATE   TIME

Each participant will have 30 minutes to fart as many times as they can. Judges will be on hand to count each fart.

I hope you can help by sponsoring me! You can pledge per fart or make a flat donation, using the form on the reverse. If you would like an audio recording of my farts sent to you, please check the box on the form. Thank you!

Fart for a Cause

Cut out this Fart-a-Thon fundraising form and use it to prank your friends and family. Make sure when they agree to sponsor you, they fill in a line in the form below.

The Smelly Truth: A man in England who was hiding from the police gave himself away when he farted. "I heard him letting rip and followed the noises to a bush," said one of the officers.

FART-A-THON

Sponsor Name	Phone Number	Pledge per Fart	Total Amount	Check to Get Audio Recording	Special Fart Requests

Emily Posterior's Farting Etiquette Guide

Many years ago, a real woman named Emily Post wrote a guide to good manners, also known as *etiquette*. She was too polite to mention farting, but this modern-day guide to pooting in public fills the gap.

Ask a friend or family member for words to fill in the blanks without letting them see the page. Then read the guide aloud.

There is nothing more embarrassing than passing gas in public. People

look at you like you're a wild _____ that just sprayed _____
                              ANIMAL   DISGUSTING LIQUID

on their favorite _____ . Unfortunately, you can't avoid farting.
                 VALUABLE OBJECT

Even _____ passes gas at least _____ times a day. But you *can*
      CELEBRITY   HIGH NUMBER

fart politely.

Here's how: First, when you sense that a smelly, _____ _____ is
                                          ADJECTIVE   NOUN

about to fly out your bottom, do not panic! Take a deep breath, turn to your

friends, and say "_____" very slowly.
                 SNACK FOOD

Then stand up, cross your _____ over your _____ ,
                      BODY PART   ANOTHER BODY PART

and balance on a(n) _____ while counting to _____ . If that
                NOUN   HIGH NUMBER

doesn't make the fart go away, quickly find a large, _____ _____ to
                                        ADJECTIVE   NOUN

sit on. It should absorb the smell. But if it doesn't, find a(n) _____ and
                                                  NOUN

a(n) _____ , and wave them around to clear the air. Then look
     NOUN

for _____ or _____ or a sleeping _____ . Smile at them
     RELATIVE   FRIEND   ANIMAL

and say, "Don't worry, dear. Everyone farts!"

Fart Your Mark

Your fart is like a fingerprint—each one is unique to you. Leave your own, special, one-of-a-kind fart on this page. Then sign and date it and keep it for posterior posterity.

I, _____ farted on this page on _____
             NAME   DATE

Signed: _____

Notes: _____

_____

_____

The
**Smelly
Truth**   The word for the rumbling sound made by gas moving around inside your stomach is *borborygmus* (pronounced *bor-buh-RIG-muss*).

Order Up at the Gas Station Café!

When Latisha Letterrip opened her new restaurant, the Gas Station Café, fart lovers the world over rejoiced. Every dish on the menu features foods known to increase flatulence.

Find all 22 of the farty foods listed in the grid and circle them. The words are hidden across, backward, up, down, and diagonally. When you're done, the letters that remain will spell out two other fart-producing foods. The answers are on page 103.

BEANS
BELL PEPPERS
BROCCOLI
CABBAGE
CAULIFLOWER
CHEESE
DRIED FRUIT
EGGS
FRIED FOOD
GARLIC
KALE

LENTILS
MILK
MUSHROOMS
OATS
PEARS
PEAS
POTATOES
RADISHES
RED MEAT
SODA
WHEAT

Why couldn't the skeleton fart in front of his friends?

He didn't have the guts.

```
D  R  B  R  S  U  C  H  E  E  S  E
R  E  W  O  L  F  I  L  U  A  C  F
I  D  S  T  I  P  H  S  I  D  A  R
E  M  M  A  T  A  E  H  W  S  E  I
D  E  U  T  N  L  S  A  S  P  R  E
F  A  S  O  E  G  G  S  S  O  G  D
R  T  H  P  L  K  A  L  E  A  A  F
U  K  R  U  S  N  A  E  B  S  R  O
I  L  O  C  C  O  R  B  R  O  L  O
T  I  O  A  T  S  A  A  T  D  I  D
S  M  M  O  N  C  E  I  O  A  C  N
S  S  R  E  P  P  E  P  L  L  E  B
```

_____ _____ & _____

The Smelly Truth The fartiest food in the world is probably the Jerusalem artichoke, a knobby root vegetable. It's loaded with inulin, a substance that makes people produce astonishing amounts of gas—"a filthie loathsome stinking winde" is how English botanist John Goodyer described it 400 years ago.

What's Your Gastrological Sign?

Some people like to read about their astrological sign to learn how the stars and the planets supposedly affect their lives. *Gastrological signs* are much more fun. They tell you how the date you were born affects your *gassy* life.

Look for your birthday in the entries below to identify your sign so you can read about your farting personality. Then write down your friends' and family's names next to their signs. Read their signs out loud to them and note if their farting style matches their gastrological sign.

Aries (MARCH 21–APRIL 19) You are energetic and turbulent, and so is your digestive system. It produces bold, attention-grabbing farts—the kind that people talk about long after the sound and smell have faded.

People I know with this sign: _____

How well does their farting match their sign? _____

Taurus (APRIL 20–MAY 20) Like the bull your sign is named for, you are a strong and consistent farter, releasing a steady, healthy flow that friends can depend on like a brand-new sewer pipe. For you, farting is more than a bodily function; it's a matter of honor.

People I know with this sign: _____

How well does their farting match their sign? _____

Gemini (MAY 21–JUNE 20)

The symbol for Gemini is a pair of twins, which explains why you have two distinct farting personas. Your gas-loving self likes to see what flatulence records you can break. Your fart-phobic side runs and hides in the bathroom at the the slightest intestinal rumble.

People I know with this sign: _____

How well does their farting match their sign? _____

Cancer (JUNE 21–JULY 22)

How you fart and how you react to other people's farts depends on your mood. When you're crabby like your sign, you'll let out a silent stink bomb. When you're in a good mood, though, you release all farts—tiny ones, rafter-shakers, and room-clearers—with an appreciative howl.

People I know with this sign: _____

How well does their farting match their sign?: _____

Leo (JULY 23–AUGUST 22)

You are a born performer who craves attention, and you discovered at a young age that farts are the perfect way to get it. You're the person who interrupts a conversation to say, "Here comes one!" and then lets loose a butt roar worthy of your sign's symbol, the lion.

People I know with this sign: _____

How well does their farting match their sign? _____

Virgo (AUGUST 23–SEPTEMBER 22) You aim for

perfection in everything you do, and breaking wind is no exception. You want every detail of a fart to be just right—it should have the rhythm and "ba-da-da-da" of a good drum solo and absolutely no odor.

People I know with this sign: _____

How well does their farting match their sign? _____

Libra (SEPTEMBER 23–OCTOBER 22) You are a kind

and considerate farter. You clench every muscle in your body trying to hold in a fart that might embarrass you or others, and you're a master of the tiny, barely audible "puff fart."

People I know with this sign: _____

How well does their farting match their sign? _____

Scorpio (OCTOBER 23–NOVEMBER 21) You

are a true leader when it comes to cutting the cheese. You show others that like all things in life, farting should be done with passion, dedication, and honesty. There is nothing you hate more than the timid, half-suppressed wimpy fart.

People I know with this sign: _____

How well does their farting match their sign? _____

Sagittarius (NOVEMBER 22–DECEMBER 21)

You are not one to sit at home farting away the hours. You love to travel, and it's not just because you like to see new places—you like to fart in them. You feel free and happy when the wind blasting from your rear end is pushing you forward to the next adventure.

People I know with this sign: _____

How well does their farting match their sign? _____

Capricorn (DECEMBER 22–JANUARY 19)

You like to feel in control of most situations and hate being caught off guard by an unexpected toot. If you could schedule every fart in your life, you would. Since you can't, you have worked hard at disguising your farts.

People I know with this sign: _____

How well does their farting match their sign? _____

Aquarius (JANUARY 20–FEBRUARY 18)

You were born a shy and quiet farter, and you will do almost anything to avoid tooting in public. But let's face it, even *you* can't prevent the occasional fartlet from slipping out. Stop worrying. Everyone farts, even Aquarians!

People I know with this sign: _____

How well does their farting match their sign? _____

Pisces (FEBRUARY 19–MARCH 20)

Your artistic side comes out in everything you do, and that includes breaking wind. For you, farting is an essential tool for creative expression, and you should never hold back. Let your gorgeous, melodic farts blast forth like trumpets.

People I know with this sign: _____

How well does their farting match their sign? _____

What to Say after Your Butt Has Spoken

When you pass gas in public, there are two main ways to avoid embarrassment: Own the fart or pretend it wasn't yours.

Either way, it helps to have something snappy to say. Here are some simple lines you can use when you want to own or deny a fart. Try these, and also make up some of your own!

THE PROUD FARTER SAYS . . .

THE CLEVER DENIER SAYS . . .

"Did you hear that flock of geese?"

"Did someone leave an egg cooking on the stove?"

"Hmmm, maybe I should change my new ringtone."

"*Somebody* didn't get the memo about reducing greenhouse gases."

"That's so not my signature scent."

"Oh dear, I think the septic tank is acting up again."

"Alexa, stop!"

"Whoever Smelt It, Dealt It"

If you get tired of the classic quip above, try these alternatives:

Whoever . . .

. . . denied it, supplied it.

. . . detected it, ejected it.

. . . policed it, released it.

. . . smelled it, expelled it.

. . . noted it, floated it.

The Smelly Truth   President Gerald Ford reportedly blamed Secret Service agents for his farts. He would loudly say things like, "Was that you? Show some class!"

Fart Madness

What's the absolute most embarrassing time and place to fart? Use this bracket to decide.

For each pairing on the left side, choose the situation you think is the most embarrassing. Write the letter for that choice on the next blank. Continue comparing the pairs until you get to the center of the chart. Your friend will do the same on the right side. You'll end up with a butt-blasting showdown!

A. On a crowded elevator

B. Very loudly in a movie theater when the heroes in the film are hiding from the bad guys and trying to be very quiet

C. Right after the teacher tells the whole class to be quiet

D. Right after you laughed at someone else for farting

E. During a game of hide-and-seek

F. In a store dressing room that someone else is waiting to use

G. When you are talking to someone you have a crush on

H. On stage during a play when you are the only one speaking

The
Worst Place

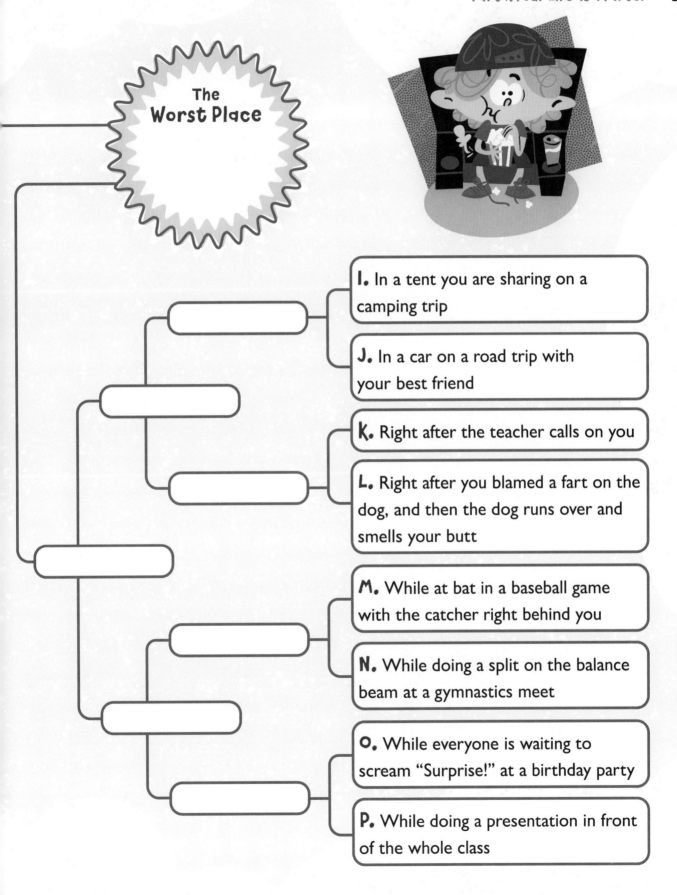

I. In a tent you are sharing on a camping trip

J. In a car on a road trip with your best friend

K. Right after the teacher calls on you

L. Right after you blamed a fart on the dog, and then the dog runs over and smells your butt

M. While at bat in a baseball game with the catcher right behind you

N. While doing a split on the balance beam at a gymnastics meet

O. While everyone is waiting to scream "Surprise!" at a birthday party

P. While doing a presentation in front of the whole class

More Madness!

Are there places that are even more embarrassing to fart in than the ones listed in the chart on the previous page? Make your own bracket by filling in the pairs below.

A.

B.

C.

D.

E.

F.

G.

H.

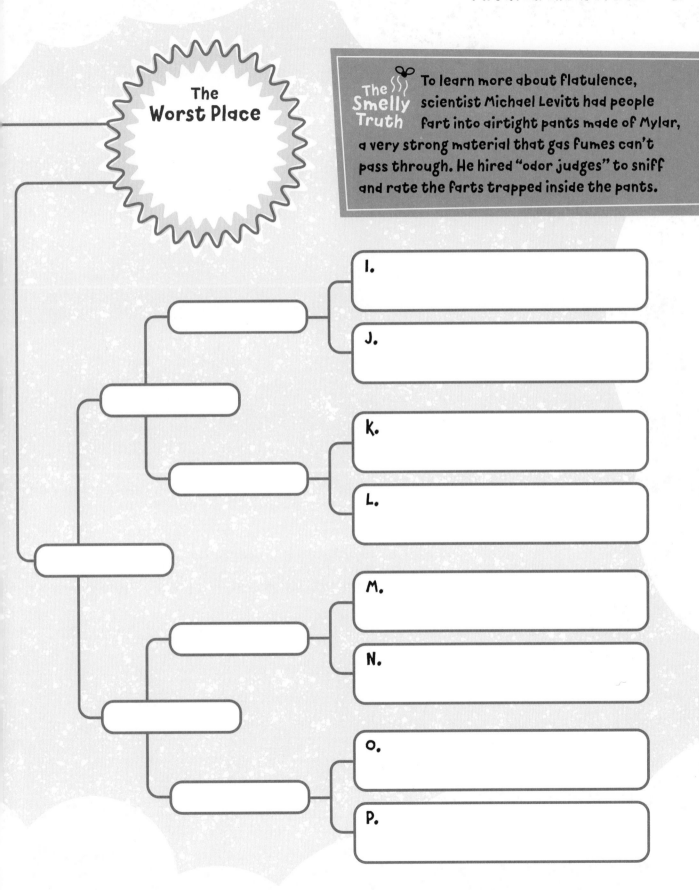

The
Worst Place

The
**Smelly
Truth**

To learn more about flatulence, scientist Michael Levitt had people fart into airtight pants made of Mylar, a very strong material that gas fumes can't pass through. He hired "odor judges" to sniff and rate the farts trapped inside the pants.

I.

J.

K.

L.

M.

N.

O.

P.

Flatulence Is the Mother of Invention

Inventors often get their inspiration for new products by noticing the little things that affect people's daily lives. Like farts, for instance. Below are six fart-related inventions, but only four of them are real. Can you guess which are the real ones? Circle the number, then check the answers on pages 103–104.

❶ Fart Pills

A French inventor claims his fart pills make your most noxious, rotten egg–scented farts come out smelling like roses. Pop one in your mouth, he says, and the next time you break wind, the scent of roses—or lilies or chocolate or ginger, if you prefer—will come wafting out your back end.

❷ Fart Reader

The Fart Reader answers the age-old question, "Who farted?" It can be programmed to recognize the signature sound, scent, and gas composition of a group of family members and friends. Then when someone farts, there is no way to escape the blame. This invention tells you instantly who the culprit is.

❸ Doggie Underwear

For dog owners who are tired of smelling their pooch's poots, an inventor designed doggie underwear with a pad containing a type of charcoal that absorbs the stink before it reaches human noses.

4 The Farting Car

For drivers who are also pranksters, a car manufacturer added a "fart mode" to one of its electric cars. You can make the seat of your choice emit fart sounds or make the turn signal and the horn go *BRAP!*

5 Flatulence in a Bottle

What if you actually *like* the smell of farts? Or you are a prankster and want to produce the smell on command without waiting for your gut to do it? A scented oil called Flatulence solves that problem. When heated, the oil perfectly mimics fart odor.

6 Farting Alarm Clock

If you want to wake up laughing every morning, this is the alarm clock for you. Instead of an electronic beep, the clock sounds a couple of short farts when it's time to get up. If you don't turn it off, the farts get louder and the clock emits a rotten-egg smell.

The Smelly Truth An amusement park in Denmark features a roller coaster called the Dog Fart. You ride in a car shaped like a character called Henry the Farting Dog and pass through a tunnel where you hear the sound of—you guessed it—farting dogs. Woof.

Your Fart Invention

Now that you've read about some ingenious ways to use farts, you can design your own fart-related invention.

Think about a flatulence problem you want to solve, or dream up a fart-related invention that's funny and entertaining.

Use the questions below to develop your idea. And don't forget to draw a picture of it. Who knows, maybe some day your idea will become a best-*smelling* product!

What is your invention called? _____

What does it do? _____

_____

_____

How does it work? _____

_____

_____

_____

What problem does it solve, if any? _____

_____

_____

_____

Why will people want this product? _____

_____

_____

_____

Draw a picture of your invention here:

The Fart That Stayed

Sometimes after a fart leaves your butt, it seems the stink lingers forever. This is the story of such a fart. Ask a friend or family member for words to fill in the blanks without letting them see the page. Then read the story out loud.

One day, _____ laid a fart at dinner. It wasn't just any old fart.
NAME OF FAMILY MEMBER

It sounded peculiar, like a(n) _____ _____ trying to sing
ADJECTIVE   SMALL ANIMAL

like _____ . It smelled weird, too, like _____ 's
NAME OF FAMOUS MUSICIAN   FRIEND'S NAME

_____ after it had been _____ in _____ for
BODY PART   -ING VERB   DISGUSTING SUBSTANCE

weeks. But the most bizarre thing of all was that it didn't fade away. It perched

on my _____ throughout dinner and made noises like a(n) _____
BODY PART   NOUN

being fried in hot _____ .
LIQUID

   We all went to bed early, hoping the fart would disappear during the night.

But in the morning we heard _____ scream. The fart was
ANOTHER FAMILY MEMBER

_____ on the bed and the room smelled like rancid _____ .
-ING VERB   FOOD YOU HATE

We tried everything we could think of to get rid of the fart. We sprayed it

with liquefied _____ and _____ . We put it in the
PLURAL NOUN   PLURAL NOUN

_____ . We jumped on it with _____ on our shoes.
KITCHEN APPLIANCE   STICKY SUBSTANCE

But it was indestructible.

   Amazingly, we began to adore that little fart. We loved how it sat on the

couch _____ all day. We even gave it
-ING VERB

a name: Stinky _____ . It's true
NAME OF FLOWER

that no one except _____
NAME OF RELATIVE

will visit us anymore. But our life is so

much more _____ .
ADJECTIVE

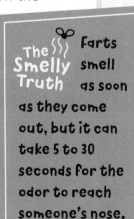

The Smelly Truth   Farts smell as soon as they come out, but it can take 5 to 30 seconds for the odor to reach someone's nose.

Out of Order

Many people keep their windy business behind the closed door of the bathroom. That makes the bathroom door a great place for a funny sign.

Carefully cut out this page and use the prank sign on the other side. Write the name of the worst farter in your house in the blank. Then tape the sign to the outside of the bathroom door and wait for someone to come along.

What happens when you're startled by a fart?

You're fartled

The Smelly Truth Beans do make people fart more, but if you eat them every day, your fart production usually drops back to normal after a few weeks.

BATHROOM CLOSED

DUE TO DANGEROUS GAS LEVELS
CAUSED BY EXCESSIVE FARTING

To file a complaint, please speak to

BATHROOM CLOSED

DUE TO DANGEROUS GAS LEVELS CAUSED BY EXCESSIVE FARTING

To file a complaint, please speak to _____.

GAS-O-METER

DANGER

MEDIUM

LOW

On the Road

We've all been on a car trip where someone (not you, of course) keeps farting like a hippopotamus on a beans-only diet. There's only one thing to do: Laugh—and then get everyone else on the road to laugh with you.

Carefully cut out this page. The next time you're on a car trip, hold the sign up to the window for other travelers to see. Use it whenever you want to bring some hilarity to the highway.

Why should you never fart in church?
Because you have to sit in your *pew.*

THIS CAR POWERED BY 100% NATURAL GAS

The Smelly Truth Astronaut John Young was first at many things. He was the first man to fly in space six times. He commanded the first space shuttle flight. And perhaps most impressive, he was the first man to fart on the moon. During the Apollo 16 mission in 1972, Young and other crewmembers had to drink tons of orange juice for health reasons. Young said the extra citrus made him extra farty.

A Fart to Remember

Every farter, whether shy or bold, can't help but congratulate themselves when they emit some truly spectacular wind. This review is for those really rare, thunder-from-down-under, five-star farts.

Ask a friend or family member for words to fill in the blanks without letting them see the page. Then read the review aloud.

The Five-Star Fart

Every _____ years, a fart is released that is so perfect, so _____ ,
___HIGH NUMBER___   ___ADJECTIVE___

that even top farter _____ is _____ with envy.
___NAME OF CELEBRITY___   ___ADJECTIVE___

The fart laid by _____ was that fart. Most farts sound like
___YOUR NAME___

_____ _____ on a toilet seat. But this fart was different. Imagine
__PLURAL NOUN__ __-ING VERB__

hearing an exploding _____ _____ collide with a(n) _____
__ADJECTIVE__ __NOUN__   __ADJECTIVE__

_____ . It was so loud and so _____ , it made my ears feel
__WILD ANIMAL__   __ADJECTIVE__

like _____ _____ . And it smelled like a mix of rotten _____
__ADJECTIVE__ __FOOD__   __PLURAL NOUN__

with _____ and _____ -year-old _____ blended
__DISGUSTING LIQUID__   __HIGH NUMBER__   __VEGETABLE__

with boiled _____ . The stench was so strong it took my
__PLURAL NOUN__

_____ away. People as far away as _____ could
__BODY PART__   __NAME OF COUNTRY__

smell it!

If I could give this fart _____ stars, I would. Even my
__HIGH NUMBER__

uncle, who farts like a bloated _____ on a(n)
__WILD ANIMAL__

_____ , cannot match this performance.
__AMUSEMENT PARK RIDE__

WORLD'S
BEST
FARTER

Part 2: Be a Fart Detective

You know it and they know it: Your family and friends fart all the time, day and night—sometimes so loudly or odoriferously they ought to be arrested. The same is true of many animals. The ferocious fossa that lives in Madagascar lays stinkers so toxic, they can make a person's eyes water! The truth is, you're exposed to so many farts from so many places in a single day, it's enough to make your head spin (and really offend your nose).

But never fear. With all the fart knowledge you're about to gain, butt sneezes from any source will be no match for you and your investigative skills. Get ready to ask the age-old question—"Who farted?"—and sniff out the answer.

The Smelly Truth Ferrets have an entertaining fart style: They often surprise themselves with their own farts. After letting a loud one rip, they will turn and peer at their butt as if to say, "Did *I* do that?"

An elderly couple was at a concert one night when the woman turned to the man and said, "I just let out a very long, silent fart. What should I do?"

The man said, "Replace the battery in your hearing aid."

Who Farted?

The Flatus family invited some relatives over for their favorite dinner of cabbage, bean, and broccoli casserole. After everyone finished eating, they were all hanging out in the living room when someone cut the cheese. Everyone behaved in the usual way—that is, by wildly overreacting, holding their noses, grimacing, and pointing their fingers to blame someone else.

Using the clues on the next page, can you figure out who farted? The answer is on page 104.

Clues:
1. The farter *is* overreacting.
2. The farter is *not* accusing someone else.
3. The farter *is* being accused.

HINT: For each clue, make a list of all the people or pets who fit the clue. Then check to see who appears on all three lists. That's the cheese cutter!

The Biggest Stinker

How do your friends and family measure up when it comes to butt music?

Use this handy chart to track the farters in your life. You'll quickly learn each person's signature style—and then you'll have evidence to present to anyone who tries to deny what they supplied. For help identifying the type of fart someone laid, consult the handy guide on page 44.

Who	When	Where	Type of Fart	Volume: 1–10	Stink Level: 1–10

The **Smelly Truth** The writer Mark Twain came up with this wonderful denial to use after you fart: "Nay, 'tis not I [yet] have broughte forth this rich o'ermastering fog, this fragrant gloom, so pray you seeke ye further."

Duration: 1-10	Melody: 1-10	Lingering Smell: 1-10	TOTAL POINTS	COMMENTS

A Guide to Common Farts

The following chart will help you identify any farts (including your own) that you encounter during your investigations.

ODOR RATING SYSTEM:

steamed broccoli = mild odor | bean burrito = moderate odor | rotten egg = strong odor

The Smelly Truth Scientists discovered in 2018 that the planet Uranus is surrounded by a giant cloud that smells like farts.

The Butt Puff: A tiny, harmless fart that's almost cute—just a quick little burst of air, the kind of fart a fairy would cut.

The Foghorn: A low moan from deep inside the gut that seems to warn that something more is on the way. Is a wild animal stuck in there? This fart is low on odor but big on weirdness.

The Trumpet: A single, loud, attention-grabbing blast that's often odorless but still plenty obnoxious.

Laughtulence: Percussive farts that pop out when you laugh.

The Jackhammer: A series of short, explosive farts released in quick succession, loud and attention-grabbing enough to wake a sleeping elephant.

The Squeaker: This high-pitched fart doesn't even seem human—it sounds like a door hinge in need of oil or a balloon animal being strangled.

The Carbonator: A soft, fizzy fart that has a disgustingly wet sound, as if you sat on a frog.

The Slow Gas Leak: When first laid, this silent fart has no scent. But half a minute later, you realize a wretched odor, like the breath of a garlic-eating dragon, is wafting out of your pants.

The Destroyer: This fart is so horrifyingly toxic that it not only clears rooms, it ends relationships between friends, relatives, even countries. Imagine the smell of dirty diapers marinating in a bucket of garbage juice in 120-degree weather. Now multiply that by 10.

In Violation of Our Noses

The next time someone lets one rip, you can slap them with this prank ticket. Carefully cut it out, fill in the blanks, and hand it to anyone whose farts are a threat to public safety.

The Smelly Truth In 1607, English lawmaker Henry Ludlow passed gas loudly during a debate in Parliament. The accidental fart was interpreted as a "no" vote, and Ludlow quickly became famous for his "tail that cried no." The farted vote even inspired a poem titled "Censure of the Parliament Fart" that became hugely popular.

Why did the man get fired from his job delivering fart awareness pamphlets?

He let one rip.

FARTING VIOLATION

The person named below is hereby summoned to appear in court to answer for farting offenses.

NAME OF ACCUSED:

_____

AGE: _____

DATE AND TIME OF VIOLATION:

_____

LOCATION OF VIOLATION :

_____

_____

DESCRIPTION OF FART:

_____

_____

DETECTION METHOD:

_____

▶ OVER

VIOLATIONS (CHECK ALL THAT APPLY):

☐ Failing to signal before farting

☐ Fart and run (leaving the room after emitting a toxic fart without providing assistance to victims)

☐ Farting while driving (with passengers in vehicle)

☐ Farting in a no-fart zone (check all that apply)

  ☐ within 5 feet of the kitchen at mealtime

  ☐ in a room with visitors present

  ☐ within 10 feet of any of the following people who have filed orders of protection against the accused for farting:

  _____

  _____

ACCUSED'S PLEA:

☐ Guilty ☐ Not guilty

☐ Too embarrassed to say

DATE AND TIME OF HEARING:

_____

HEARING LOCATION:

☐ Living Room ☐ Kitchen

☐ Outside, just to be safe

SIGNATURE OF ARRESTING OFFICER:

_____

Cut out this farting summons, fill out both sides, and slap it on a friend or family member who breaks some law-breaking wind.

Time to Check Your Gas-O-Meter

Let your friends and family know that their dangerously high fart-gas emissions are getting attention with this prank notice!

Carefully cut out this form. Fill in the front with your family's or friend's name. Then leave it on their front door for someone to find. Make sure they fill in the back.

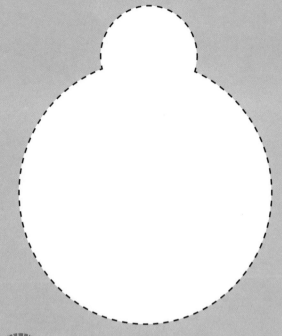

 **CENTRAL GAS**
COMPANY

NOTICE

SORRY WE MISSED YOU!

Customer name:

_____

Our company monitors household gas emissions. We came by today because our meters indicate that the amount of human-source methane being emitted by your household is cause for concern. Methane is a component of digestive gas.

The methane levels for your house are currently:

☑ extremely dangerous ☐ somewhat dangerous

☐ unpleasant but safe ☐ normal

To help us determine why your family is producing so much gas, please answer the questions on the reverse side of this card and leave it on your doorknob for pickup. We will contact you to discuss measures you can take to get your gas emissions under control and plan for evacuation if necessary.

(Turn over to complete this form.)

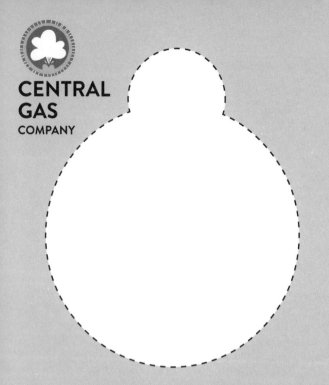

CENTRAL GAS COMPANY

Carefully cut out this prank gas company form, fill out the other side, and hang it on a friend or family member's door. Alert them to their dangerous fart gas production!

PLEASE ANSWER EVERY QUESTION.

Name: _____

Number of people in household: _____

Esimated total number of farts released by household members on an average day: _____

Have you noticed a recent increase in fart production?

☐ Yes ☐ No

If so, can you explain it? _____

To help us assess how severe the gas emissions in your house are, please check any conditions you have observed during the last two weeks:

☐ Your house smells really, really bad. Worse than usual.

☐ Family members have started sleeping with their head out the window.

☐ Plants are drooping or dying even though you water them regularly.

☐ Pets refuse to come inside.

☐ Mail carriers and delivery people wear noseclips when approaching the door.

☐ Friends and relatives turn down invitations to visit and give lame excuses.

Please add any other observations that may indicate excessive fart-gas emissions: _____

_____

Thank you for your assistance. We will contact you shortly to discuss what action is necessary.

Test Your Fart Smarts

There's a lot more to know about farts than simply who cut one. Take this quiz to find out what your flatulence IQ is. Then turn to pages 104–105 to see how you scored.

1 **Which of the following makes farts smell bad?**

A. Drinking a lot of soda or bubbly water

B. Eating foods (such as meat or asparagus) that contain sulfur, a chemical that smells like rotten eggs

C. Holding a fart in for a long time

BRRRAP!

3 **In which of these places do people tend to fart more?**

A. Classrooms

B. Elevators

C. Airplanes

POP!

2 **True or false:** If you hold in a fart for a long time, it can end up coming out your mouth.

TOOOOOT!

4 **True or false:** You can continue to fart after you die.

PFFFT!

BRRRAHOOO!

6 True or false: Eating vanilla- or peppermint-flavored foods makes your farts smell sweeter.

POP!

5 During the early years of the United States space program, scientists studied the farts of astronauts because:

A. They were worried that if the smell of a fart got trapped inside astronauts' space suits, they would be too grossed out to work.

B. They were concerned that the gases released by farts could be a fire hazard in the sealed environment of the spacecraft.

C. They wanted to know if farts sound the same in outer space as they do on Earth.

7 Which of the following allows you to see a fart?

A. Farting underwater
B. Farting during a full moon
C. Farting onto a white wall

8 True or false: The gases in people's farts are major contributors to global warming.

BRRRAP!

PFFFT!

The Smelly Truth   The first recorded joke, written 4,000 years ago, was a fart joke.

It's Time to Take the G.A.T.!

That's right—the Gassy Animal Test! Test your knowledge of furry, finned, and flying farters. Then turn to pages 105–107 to see how you did.

1 **Which animal makes the loudest farts?**

A. Dog

B. Zebra

C. Frog

2 **Which animal never farts?**

A. Bird

B. Spider

C. Bat

3 **True or false:** An airplane that was transporting goats had to make an emergency landing because the goats farted and burped out so much gas they set off the fire alarm.

4 **Which two animals share the record for smelliest farts?**

A. Seal and sea lion

B. Gorilla and chimpanzee

C. Hippopotamus and bear

5 **The Sonoran coral snake uses its farts to:**

A. Clean its nest
B. Frighten predators
C. Entertain its young

6 **Which animal farts without making any sound?**

A. Rabbit
B. Snake
C. Millipede

7 **True or false:** There is a species of insect whose farts are truly silent but deadly and are used to kill prey.

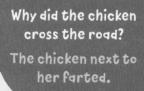

Why did the chicken cross the road?

The chicken next to her farted.

8 Which animal population emits the most methane, a greenhouse gas, through farting?

A. Cows

B. Termites

C. Dogs

9 A herring uses its farts to:

A. Communicate with other herring

B. Propel itself through the water

C. Avoid getting caught by fishermen

10 Sloths produce smelly digestive gas, but unlike most mammals, they don't fart out their butts. How does the gas get out?

A. It comes out their ears.

B. It comes out with their breath.

C. The sloth's belly button has a release valve.

The Smelly Truth   Farting is a matter of life and death for the Bolson pupfish. It eats aquatic plants called algae and ends up swallowing gas bubbles emitted by the plants. The gas builds up in the fish's intestines and makes the fish float to the surface, where it can be seen and gobbled up by birds. Luckily, after a fart or two, the fish sinks back down to safety.

Butt Burps and Cheek Squeaks

You've probably heard popular fart slang like "cut the cheese." There are hundreds of other words for fart, from "wallpaper peeler" for extremely pungent stink bombs to "butt trumpet" and "bowel howl" for extra-loud farts. There's even an expression for a tuneful toot: "Mozart fart," named after the famous composer.

Use your fart detective skills to find the slang expressions listed below in the grid on the next page. The words are hidden across, backward, up, down, and diagonally. When you're done, the remaining letters will spell out the punch line to a joke. The answers are on page 107.

List of Fart Phrases

AIR BISCUIT

BLURP

BUTT BURP

CHEEK SQUEAK

FARTKIN (a tiny fart)

FIZZLE (a silent fart)

LAY AN EGG

ODOR MOTOR

PANT RIPPER

POOT

RUMP ROAR

SBD (silent but deadly)

SQUEEZE CHEESE

STINKBURGER

SWAMP GAS

TAIL TALK

THUNDER BUTT

TOOT

TROUSER COUGH

Why did the stock market investor keep trying to hold in his farts?

He heard the price of gas was about to go up.

```
T H G U O C R E S U O R T
H K L A T L I A T R E K B
R U M P R O A R T O T A R
T O S R S S N S U T I E E
O A I U D I T A B O U U G
O O C B K F U G R M C Q R
P A N T R I P P E R S S U
T M R T O Z R M D O I K B
R A O U E Z U A N D B E K
F O S B D L L W U O R E N
T C H E E E B S H S I H I
G G E N A Y A L T E A C T
E S E E H C E Z E E U Q S
```

The joke: Why did the worker in the sandwich shop fart so much?

___ ____ ____ __ ___ ____ _____.

Farty Friends for Life

Friends who fart together, stay together! You've shared jokes, secrets, class notes, books, and games with your best bud. Now commemorate your friendship by farting on this page together. Don't forget to sign, date, and describe your best-friend farts so you'll remember all the good gassy times you've had.

_____ farted here on _____ .
                NAME   DATE

Brief description of the fart: _____

_____

                                    _____
                                                    SIGNATURE

_____ farted here on _____ .
NAME   DATE

Brief description of the fart: _____

_____

_____
                                                          SIGNATURE

Breaking Wind around the World

Farting is a universal language. No matter where you go in the world, when someone passes gas, you instantly recognize the sound—and the smell. But the *words* people use to say "fart" vary a lot, depending on the language they speak.

This guide will help you track farters all over the globe. *And* you can impress your friends and family with your awesome language skills.

Language	Word for "Fart"	Pronunciation
Arabic	ضطة	ZTHURR-tah
French	pet	PAY
German	Furz	FOORTZ
Hindi	अपान वायु	ah-PAHN VY-you
Italian	scoreggia	sco-REH-jyah
Japanese	屁	AY
Korean	방귀	BAHNG-GWEE
Mandarin	屁	PEE
Norwegian	promp	PROMP
Portuguese	pum	POOM
Russian	пердун	pare-DOHN
Spanish	pedo	PAY-doh
Swahili	jamba	JAHM-bah
Tagalog	utot	oo-TAWT
Vietnamese	cái địt	ky-DEE

The Smelly Truth In German, the word *fahrt* is pronounced just like *fart*, but it means "journey." So if you want to wish someone a nice trip in Germany, say, "Have a good fahrt." In Norway, *fart* means "speed," so if a cop pulls you over for driving *full fart*, he's referring to your high speed, not your high-quality toots.

A Letter from the Dog

After years of being blamed for people's farts, dogs are rising up to say: Stop!

Ask a friend or family member for words to fill in the blanks without letting them see the page. Then read the letter aloud, on behalf of dogs everywhere.

Dear Humans,

Buddy was just a six-month-old puppy when the blaming began. He was a

cute, _____ -faced beagle- _____ mix who loved the _____
        ADJECTIVE   NOUN   FRIEND'S LAST NAME

family and thought they loved him right back. But then one night at dinner, someone let

out a fart that smelled like rotting _____ . "That wasn't me, that was
                                      FOOD YOU HATE

Buddy," said the farter. Buddy couldn't believe his _____ ears! How could
                                                     ADJECTIVE

they pin this on him? He knew who released all _____ farts every day.
                                                HIGH NUMBER

_____ 's farts smelled like _____ vomit. _____ 's
FAMILY MEMBER   WILD ANIMAL   ANOTHER FAMILY MEMBER

were louder than 70 _____ .
                    PLURAL MUSICAL INSTRUMENT

Buddy is not alone. He is one of the _____ million dogs who are
                                     HIGH NUMBER

wrongly blamed for humans' _____ gas *every day*. We appreciate the love
                           ADJECTIVE

and loyalty that exist between dogs and humans. But the fart blaming must stop.

Here's how you can help:

• If you *must* blame someone for your farts, try _____ . We all know they
                                                 NAME OF FRIEND

fart like a(n) _____ -pound _____ .
              HIGH NUMBER   WILD ANIMAL

• Learn to admit to your _____ -smelling farts. We know you do
                         DISGUSTING FOOD

it, especially when you are _____ in the _____ .
                           -ING VERB   PLACE

Sincerely,

Dogs Everywhere

Find the Beastly Farters

Can you sniff out all 14 of the farting animals lurking in the grid? The names are hidden across, backward, up, down, and diagonally. Circle all the names. When you're done, the remaining letters will spell out the punch line to a joke. The answers are on page 107.

Farting Animals

CORAL SNAKE	MILLIPEDE
FERRET	PUPFISH
FOSSA	SEA LION
GOAT	SEAL
GORILLA	TERMITE
HERRING	TERRIER
LACEWING	ZEBRA

The Smelly Truth When Joseph Pujol was growing up in France, he discovered he could pull air in through his butt and then fart it out. He put this rare talent to work as an adult by performing on stage as "Le Pétomane," which means *Fartomaniac.* He tooted out songs, imitated animals, even blew out candles with his farts. Audiences loved him, and in 1894, he was the highest-paid performer in France!

How did the boy learn to fart loudly?
He watched a toot-torial.

E K A N S L A R O C
F A R G N I R R E H
T A L L I R O G R E
H S E A L I O N E T
S S E R D A A I I I
I E R B T A S W R M
F A I E N B S E R R
P L O Z W S O C E E
U T E R R E F A T T
P E D E P I L L I M

The joke: What happened to the family that ate only beans and Skittles?

The answer: They _ _ _ _ _ _ _   _ _ _ _ _ _ _ _ _.

Part 3: Every Day Is Fart Day!

The world can be divided into people who think farting is rude and embarrassing and those who think it's the funniest, most wonderful thing a person can do. Guess which people have more fun? The ones who know how to celebrate flatulence in all its thunderous, putrid splendor! Having fun with farts is as easy as lifting a butt cheek. Do these activities with a friend, or lots of them, or your family, or gather *all* your squeaky peeps together for a blowout farty party.

> **What do you call a dinosaur fart?**
> A blast from the past.

Throw a Farty Party!

Get all your gassiest friends and family together for a fun-filled fart fest. Use this planner to make your celebration truly fartastic.

1 Decide the basics (and talk everything over with an adult, of course).

What day will the party be? _____

What time of day will it be? Will it be a sleepover? _____

Where will it be? Indoors? Outdoors? _____

Who will you invite?

_____ _____ _____ _____

_____ _____ _____ _____

_____ _____ _____ _____

2 Pick a name or theme for your fart party: _____

3 Make the invitations. You can design your own invitation on paper or digitally, or cut out the one on the next page and fill it in. Make copies and deliver or mail them to your friends and family.

4 Decide about decorations. Here are two ideas:

* Make large drawings of farts (see page 86) in all different colors and put them on the walls.
* Make balloon clouds to hang around the room to look like lingering farts.
* Add your ideas here:

_____

_____

5 Snacks

A couple of days before the party, decide what farty food you will serve, and leave time to shop for the ingredients and make the snacks. (You can find ideas for easy-to-make farty snacks on page 67.)

6 Games and Contests

You can find ideas for farty games and contests beginning on pages 68, 84, and 98. Write down your own ideas for games or activities here:

_____

_____

Now you're ready! Let the flatulence fly!

The Smelly Truth One of the United States's founding fathers, Benjamin Franklin, wrote an essay called "Fart Proudly" in which he jokingly proposed that scientists should find ways to make farts smell better.

The Smelly Truth: A researcher found that the whoopee cushion fart noise that people find funniest has a whinnying sound and lasts a long time—about 7 seconds.

When: _____

Where: _____

What: Farting games, farty food, fart contests! All farts, all the time!

What to bring: Your butt, your digestive system, nose clips, a bean dish to share, and your best farts!

RSVP: _____
EMAIL OR PHONE

A Recipe for Farting

These fart-promoting snacks are guaranteed to make you and your friends and family gloriously gassy. Serve them for a rootin' tootin' good time at your farty party—or anytime you want to gas up.

Ask an adult to help you in the kitchen.

BUTT BONGO BEAN DIP

BUTT BONGO BEAN DIP

INGREDIENTS

1 (15-ounce) can pinto beans

1 tablespoon white vinegar

3 slices canned jalapeño pepper

A pinch of salt

½ teaspoon sugar

¼ teaspoon onion powder

⅛ teaspoon garlic powder

⅛ teaspoon ground cayenne

FOR SERVING

Tortilla chips

Cauliflower

Broccoli

Green peppers

DIRECTIONS

1 Rinse and drain the beans. Put them in a food processor or blender with the other ingredients.

2 Blend until smooth.

3 Serve in a bowl with tortilla chips and bite-size pieces of raw cauliflower, broccoli, and green peppers for maximum gas effect.

FRUITY TOOTIES

Dried fruit and certain fresh fruits are the farter's friend.

Fill small bowls with lots of dried apricots, peaches, prunes, and raisins.

Serve fresh apples and pears, too.

BUBBLE TROUBLE

Serve soda or carbonated water to drink. All those air bubbles will get you poppin'.

Farting Games

These games are perfect for a farty party. But they're also fun to play in between parties, whenever you find yourself with fart-loving friends.

PASS THE GAS

This game is like tag with farts. It works best if the players are very farty, so consider serving chili, burritos, or another bean-filled dish before you play.

Here's how the game works: When someone farts, they touch another player and yell, "Pass the gas!" Then the player who got touched is "it" and has to "pass the gas" to someone else by touching them and making a fart noise. You can shield yourself by intercepting someone's hand with your elbow.

THE DEADLY FARTER

This game is best played at night or in a room that can be darkened by curtains or shades. You need five or more players and a slip of paper for each player.

1 Before you begin, mark one of the slips of paper with the letter F for Farter. Mark another one with the letter D for Detective. Leave the rest blank. Fold the slips and pass them out. The person who gets the D must tell the group, but everyone else keeps silent.

2 Now turn out the lights. Everyone except the Detective hides. Then the Farter sneaks up on a hiding player, makes a fart sound, and runs away. The victim yells "EWWWWW!" and then falls over, passed out from the fart.

3 With the lights back on, everyone gathers around the victim. The Detective tries to figure out who the Farter is by asking the victim and other players questions about what they saw or who they think did it. Everyone must answer the questions truthfully *except* the Farter. The Farter can lie except if asked directly whether they are the Farter—then they must confess. The Detective has three chances to identify the Farter. If the Detective fails, the Farter wins the game.

DOORKNOB

This game can be played anytime someone farts. You only need two people to play but can include more. The fartier the better!

When one person farts, the other people immediately say, "Doorknob! No safety! No rebounds! No self-service!" Then they start tickling the farter, and they don't stop until the farter touches a doorknob. The farter can avoid being tickled at the start by saying *one* of the words "safety," "rebounds," or "self-service" before the others do. If the farter says "safety," no one can tickle the farter. If the farter says "rebounds," the farter gets to tickle the others until they touch a doorknob. "Self-service" means the farter will tickle themself but is safe from the group.

FIND YOUR FART NAME AND MOTTO

Everyone should have a fart name. It's fun to create methane monikers together with your friends and family at a party or anytime. Use one or all of the methods below, filling in the blanks for each person. Then pick the names you like best.

1 Your favorite flower + your favorite color + a type of fart*

*See page 44 if you need ideas.

YOUR FAVORITE FLOWER	+ YOUR FAVORITE COLOR	+ A TYPE OF FART

2 Name of your pet (or a pet you know) + first syllable of your last name + "fart"

NAME OF A PET	+ FIRST SYLLABLE OF YOUR LAST NAME	+ THE WORD "FART"

3 A word that decribes today's weather + your favorite fruit + "fizzle"

A WORD THAT DESCRIBES TODAY'S WEATHER	+ YOUR FAVORITE FRUIT	+ THE WORD "FIZZLE"

Happy Fart Day!

Sometimes you need a reason to celebrate someone else. But you never need a reason to celebrate a fart! Those honking blasts and squeaky beeps happen all the time, which means every day is Fart Day!

Use the card on the next page to wish someone a happy Fart Day anytime you want. Here's how:

> **Why did the fart miss graduation?**
>
> It got expelled.

1 **Carefully cut out the card along the dotted line.**

2 **Fold the card in half so the poem is on the inside.**

3 **Write the recipient's name on the inside (Dear _____), and sign your name.**

4 **Don't forget to fart on the card before you give it!**

The Smelly Truth About 400 years ago, doctors in London, England, wrongly believed that foul-smelling vapors in the air caused the deadly illness known as the bubonic plague. Their solution? They told patients to collect their farts in jars and inhale the odor whenever they thought they had breathed foul air from outside. The idea was that you could cancel out the bad effects of one smelly vapor by inhaling another. Of course, fart smelling did nothing to prevent disease. Not to mention, it's not easy to capture farts in a jar!

> **Why should you never fart on an elevator?**
>
> It's wrong on so many levels.

HAPPY FART!

FARTED

Thinking of you.

Fartwell Card Company
Butte, Montana

On this page so clean and bright
I laid a fart, on the right.
It's a gift you'll love, I think.
Please enjoy the special stink!

Dear _____

I farted here.

Love _____

Fart-a-Pella

You can make your own butt-music beat on command without any equipment other than your mouth, elbows, hands, and armpit. Try each of these methods and rate the results.

MOUTH FARTS

The easiest way to mimic the sound of breaking wind is to stick out your tongue and blow, sometimes called *blowing a raspberry*. You're probably already a pro at this, but if not, here's how you do it.

1 Stick your tongue out just a little so it rests on your lower lip but doesn't go beyond it.

2 Press down a little with your teeth and blow. You should hear a nice, wet fart sound.

3 Experiment to get different sounds. If you keep your lips tight around your tongue so only a little air can get out, then fill your cheeks with air and blow, you'll get a very authentic sound. Sticking your tongue out farther will vary the sounds.

Your rating for mouth farts:

On a scale of 1–5 (with 5 being highest), how realistic were these sounds? _____

On a scale of 1–5, how funny were they? _____

What kind of fart noises did you make? _____

How many people were fooled by the sound? _____

The Smelly Truth Humans are not the only creatures that make fart noises with their mouths. Scientists have seen orangutans blow raspberries as they prepare their nests at bedtime. No one knows why they do it, but perhaps, like humans, they find it funny.

ELBOW FARTS

Who knew the inside of your elbow was such a useful place? Put your mouth there and blow hard, and you'll get to hear some excellent fart sounds.

Your rating for elbow farts:

On a scale of 1–5 (with 5 being highest), how realistic were these sounds? _____

On a scale of 1–5, how funny were they? _____

What kind of fart noises did you make? _____

How many people were fooled by the sound? _____

HAND FARTS

This method takes some practice, but it's worth the effort, especially if you want to make those high-pitched farts known as cheek squeakers. Here's how you do it:

1 Put your hands together, palm to palm, with your fingers wrapped around the opposite hand.

2 Push your palms together hard, then release them slightly. Continue doing this at a steady pace until you hear a fart sound. Experiment by changing the speed of your hands or loosening the grip of your fingers. The goal is to create a pocket of air between your palms and then squeeze all the air out to form a seal. When you separate your palms, the seal breaks and makes a nice fart sound.

Your rating for hand farts:

On a scale of 1–5 (with 5 being highest), how realistic were these sounds? _____

On a scale of 1–5, how funny were they? _____

What kind of fart noises did you make? _____

How many people were fooled by the sound? _____

ARMPIT FARTS

If you don't mind sticking your hand in your armpit, this method will make people laugh not just for the fart sounds, but for how funny you look flapping like a chicken.

You'll need access to your armpit, so wear a tank top or a shirt that buttons down the front, with the top few buttons undone. Here's what you do:

1 Make sure your hands are clean and dry. Cup your left hand and place it under your right armpit. Press firmly so you create a tight seal between your hand and your armpit.

2 Now bend and lift your right elbow and squeeze it down very quickly. Keep doing this until you start to hear fart sounds. It will take some practice and you may need to change the position of your hand and adjust the speed of your flapping arm. You don't need to make a big movement with your right arm. Small but fast squeezes will do the trick. (You may want to wash your hands after.)

Your rating for armpit farts:

On a scale of 1–5 (with 5 being highest), how realistic were these sounds? _____

On a scale of 1–5, how funny were they? _____

What kind of fart noises did you make? _____

How many people were fooled by the sound? _____

The **Smelly Truth** 🦟 Gerry Phillips has taken hand farts to a whole new level. He can play entire songs, including the theme from Super Mario Bros., using just the fart sounds he makes with the palms of his hands.

On Your Mark, Get Set, Pfffft!

Who can make the best fart sound effects among your friends and family? There's only one way to find out. Hold a farting contest! Here's how:

1 Gather all the contestants together and give them some time to practice the sound effects on pages 75–77.

2 Ask someone who is not competing to be the judge. They can use the scorecard on the right or make their own.

3 Now let the farting begin! For each event, announce the contestants one by one. Let them each fart three times and ask the judge to rate those farts on a scale of 1 (weak) to 10 (fabulously fartastic). Write down just the highest score.

4 Add up the scores for each contestant in all the events. Whoever gets the highest total is the winner.

What is the sharpest thing in the world?

A fart. It goes right through your pants and doesn't leave a hole.

FART CONTEST SCORECARD

EVENTS	Scores for _____ NAME	Scores for _____ NAME	Scores for _____ NAME	Scores for _____ NAME	Scores for _____ NAME
Mouth Fart					
Elbow Fart					
Hand Fart					
Armpit Fart					
TOTAL POINTS					

What do you call a teacher who never farts in front of other people?

A private tooter.

Slime Farts

Slime has lots of excellent properties. It's gooey and gross and fun to play with. But did you know that you can use it to make delightfully convincing fart noises? Here's how:

MAKE THE SLIME

WHAT YOU NEED:
- 1 cup (8 ounces) of washable clear glue
- ½ cup (4 ounces) of water
- Nontoxic squeeze gel color (optional; use whatever color you like)
- Liquid starch
- Medium bowl
- Popsicle stick or other disposable stirrer
- 8-ounce jar or cup

WHAT YOU DO:
1. Pour the glue into the bowl.
2. Add the water to the glue and stir very well.
3. If you are using gel color, add 2 drops and stir until it's blended in.
4. Add 2 tablespoons of liquid starch and stir well.
5. Repeat step 4 and stir a lot. Then add and stir even more. The slime should start to thicken. If it doesn't get thick enough, add more liquid starch in tiny amounts and stir until it's nice and thick and holds together in one big glob.
6. Remove the slime from the bowl and start kneading it with your hands. Pull it apart, then fold it into a lump, then pull it apart again. Keep kneading it and squeezing it until it becomes a nice smooth ball of slime.
7. Put the ball of slime in the jar or cup. You might have to tear some off if you have too much. You want the jar to be filled to just over its top with slime.

8. Push your index finger or two fingers straight into the middle of the slime. You'll hear farting sounds as your finger compresses the slime.
9. Remove your hand, fold the excess slime at the top of the jar back inside, and push again to create even more farts.

Now you have a portable farting machine you can take anywhere!

Your rating for slime farts:

On a scale of 1–5 (with 5 being highest), how realistic were these sounds? _____

On a scale of 1–5, how funny were they? _____

What kind of fart noises did you make?

_____

How many people were fooled by the sound? _____

Whoopee for the Whoopee Cushion!

When it comes to making fart sounds, there's probably nothing as reliably hilarious as a whoopee cushion. The famous pink rubber pillow produces an embarrassingly juicy "raspberry" fart sound when a victim unwittingly plops down on it. This best-selling prank was not the first fart gag, but it's one of the best. Invented in 1930 by workers at a rubber company in Toronto, Canada, early models were green and had a wooden mouth. Soon the company switched to making the entire device out of pink rubber. They called it a "poo poo cushion" and the "boop-boop a doop" before settling on the name "whoopee cushion" in 1932. The rest is history— sofas and chairs have never been the same.

What recently discovered continent is covered with ice and has a gassy scent?

Antfarctica

Which explorer sailed around the world powered by the wind from his farts?

Fartinand Magellan

The Smelly Truth It's said that hundreds of years ago, court jesters in Europe used inflated pig bladders to make fart noises, a very early version of the whoopee cushion.

QUIET! Testing in progress.

Poot Poetry

Farts and poetry go together like beans and cabbage. For years, kids have driven parents crazy by chanting a rhyme called "Beans, Beans, the Musical Fruit." Here are the words to this celebration of the fartiest food:

Beans, beans, the musical fruit,

The more you eat, the more you toot.

The more you toot, the better you feel.

So let's have beans with every meal.

Try writing your own rhyme in praise of farting. You can make one up from scratch. Or you can follow the pattern of the "Musical Fruit" rhyme but use different words. Here's an example:

Beef, pork, sausage link,

The more you eat, the more you stink.

The more you stink, the more people scram,

So make every meal beef, pork, or ham.

For help getting started, here is a list of fart-related words:

toot, poot, fart, break wind, cut one, cut the cheese, pass gas, smell, stink, stench, reek, rotten egg, odor, putrid, gag, howl, blast, burst, laugh, giggle, shriek, scream, flee

Write your finished farting rhyme here:

_____

_____

_____

_____

The Smelly Truth

January 7 is National Pass Gas Day in the United States. Conveniently, it's the day after National Bean Day.

Fart Haiku

Haiku poems have three lines, they almost never rhyme, and they always follow these rules:

Line 1 has five syllables.

Line 2 has seven syllables.

Line 3 has five syllables.

You can write haiku poems about anything—including flatulence. Here are two examples:

Silent but deadly,

skunk smell invades the classroom.

No more burritos.

How did I do that?

High, squeaky violin sound.

Musical behind.

Try writing your own haiku that expresses something you've observed about farts—yours or someone else's!

_____

_____

_____

_____

_____

_____

The Smelly Truth Farts have inspired poets to write silly verse for centuries. One example comes from British author Spike Milligan, who included these lines in a poem from his book *Silly Verse for Kids*: "Maveric Prowles had rumbling bowles that thundered in the night. It shook the bedrooms all around and gave the folks a fright."

Let's Get Ready to Rumble!

If you pride yourself on your farts and like hearing other talented farters perform, the World Flatulence Championship is the place for you.

   Ask a friend or family member for words to fill in the blanks without letting them see the page. Then read the script aloud in your best sports-announcer voice.

It's a(n) _____ day here at the _____ National
            ADJECTIVE   FIRST AND LAST NAME OF PET

Stadium, where we are gathered for the World Flatulence Championship. We're

watching the finals of the Expressive Farting Pairs event. The favorites,

_____ and _____ ,
FIRST AND LAST NAME OF ONE RELATIVE   FIRST AND LAST NAME OF ANOTHER RELATIVE

just scored _____ for farting while _____ with their heads in
            HIGH NUMBER   -ING VERB

a(n) _____ . That _____ performance will be hard to beat. But let's
      NOUN   ADJECTIVE

watch _____ and _____ try. _____
       NAME OF FRIEND   NAME OF ANOTHER FRIEND   NAME OF FIRST FRIEND

learned to fart from their father, who literally blew the roof off the _____
                                                                        VEGETABLE

Arena with their _____ , _____ -decibel fart. And _____
                  ADJECTIVE   HIGH NUMBER   NAME OF SECOND FRIEND

learned from their mother, who propelled a(n) _____ -foot _____
                                               HIGH NUMBER   NOUN

across _____ with a single fart. They will fart to the tune
        NAME OF A COUNTRY

of _____ while hanging from an inflatable _____ .
    FAVORITE SONG   NOUN

Here they go. . . . Wow! These two fart like a(n) _____ that ate
                                                   WILD ANIMAL

too much _____ and sat on a hot _____ . And the
          DISGUSTING SUBSTANCE   NOUN

smell! It's like rotten _____ cooked in _____ . Now here
                         VEGETABLE   DISGUSTING LIQUID

come the scores. Our final contestants won the gold medal! What _____
                                                                 ADJECTIVE

farters! The best since _____ and _____ farted
                         CELEBRITY   ANOTHER CELEBRITY

the entirety of _____ .
                 NAME OF MUSICAL

The Art of the Fart

You can make any picture a lot funnier by adding a fart. Fortunately, farts are very easy to draw. All it takes is three straight lines and two curvy lines.

Here's how you do it:

1 Draw three straight lines at an angle. That's the fart being ejected.

2 Add a loopy line that's three half circles touching each other. That's the cloud of fart gas.

3 Add one more little curved line, like an eyelash, in the middle of the cloud to make it look three-dimensional.

4 That's it! You can draw farts just like this all day. Then hang them up and call it your Fart Gallery.

Experiment with drawing all different types of farts on the next page. You can add flies flying around the cloud to show it's a stinky fart. Or you can indicate sound by drawing a lot of small fart clouds in a row. *Rat-a-tat-tat.* Get creative. Draw a fart so crazy it has never been released by a human butt!

The Smelly Truth An Australian musician named Loz Blain composed a symphony based on an extremely musical fart that he had recorded to send to his brother as a joke. The symphony quickly went viral and has been used to teach music to middle schoolers.

How is success like a fart?
It only bothers people when it's not their own.

My Fart Gallery

Family Fart Portrait

You've probably taken hundreds of family photos to document vacations, holidays, and everything in between. But now you can preserve your family's butt blasts for future generations to appreciate!

Draw a circle or fart cloud for each person in your family on these pages. Then invite each family member to deposit a fart on their spot and add their signature and date.

The Smelly Truth For years people have blamed cow farts for contributing to climate change. It's true that cows emit large amounts of methane, a harmful greenhouse gas. But it turns out that most of it exits from the front end, as burps, thanks to the cow's digestive process, which goes roughly like this: chew, digest, regurgitate, repeat. So go ahead and blame the cow, but not the farts.

Welcome to the _____ Fart Museum!
ADJECTIVE

Imagine visiting a museum that has famous farts on display instead of paintings. Ask a friend or family member for words to fill in the blanks without letting them see the page. Then read the script aloud in your best tour-guide voice.

Welcome to the _____ Museum of Farts. My name is _____ DeGasse
YOUR LAST NAME   FLOWER

and I will be your guide today. We'll start with the biggest, most _____ fart
                                                              ADJECTIVE

in our collection. It was laid in _____ on _____ more than
                                  YOUR TOWN AND STATE   YOUR BIRTHDAY

200 years ago, but it smells like it was emitted just _____ seconds ago.
                                                      SMALL NUMBER

The fartist ate boiled _____ at every meal and liked to fart wearing only
                       PLURAL NOUN

_____ .
ITEM OF CLOTHING (PLURAL)

   Next on our tour is the famed _____ Fart. Some people say it smells
                                 NAME OF CELEBRITY

like _____ , but I think it smells more like old _____ .
     KIND OF DESSERT   ANIMAL BODY PART (PLURAL)

They say that when it was laid, it sounded like _____ _____ playing
                                                HIGH NUMBER PLURAL ANIMAL

the _____ in a cave.
    MUSICAL INSTRUMENT

   In this room we have the rarest, most _____ fart in the museum, called
                                         ADJECTIVE

the SmartFart. This fart can _____ , and it can also _____ !
                             VERB   VERB

   Our tour is over now, but please visit our _____
                                              ADJECTIVE

gift shop, where you can buy fart-covered

_____ and _____ and fart-
ITEM OF CLOTHING   PLURAL NOUN

infused _____ .
        SNACK FOOD

The Smelly Truth An old term for a fart sound you make with your mouth is a "Bronx cheer." The Bronx is a part of New York City where, 100 years ago, residents were not known for their politeness.

FART THIS WAY

Create Your Own Fart Museum

As far as we know, no city anywhere in the world has a real fart museum. You can do something about that sorry situation by creating your own collection of rare and unusual farts.

WHAT YOU NEED:

- Markers
- Paper
- 4 or more empty, clear glass jars with the labels removed. The older they look, the better.
- Scissors
- Tape

OPTIONAL:

- Smelly cheese
- Cauliflower
- Worcestershire sauce or brown food coloring

WHAT YOU DO:

1 Make a sign

Choose a name for your museum and use the markers and paper to make a sign. You can call it something simple, like the Fart Museum, or something fancier, like the Royal Museum of Rare and Historic Farts.

2 Label the jars

You can use the labels on page 93 for your specimens. Carefully cut out your favorites, write in names and dates where needed, and tape them to the outsides of the jars. Or make your own labels.

3 Set up your museum

Find a shelf, bookcase, or desk where you can display your collection of farts. Hang your sign above the collection and invite a friend or family member for a guided tour. You can even charge admission—or emission—if you want.

4 Optional: Add fart smells

If you have lids for the jars, you can try adding farty smells to the jars. Let visitors to the museum take a quick sniff when you crack open the jars. Here's how to make the smells:

- Place a piece of smelly cheese at the bottom of a jar, put the lid on, and wait for the smell to build up.

- Use food coloring or Worcestershire sauce to dye a few small pieces of cauliflower brown so they look fart-like. Put them in a microwave-safe bowl with a tiny bit of water and (with an adult's help) microwave them for 1 minute. Use a spoon to transfer the hot cauliflower pieces to a jar, close the lid, and wait for the smell to develop.

The Smelly Truth   The official record for the longest fart is 2 minutes and 42 seconds.

Museum of Rare and Historic Farts

Cut out these labels and tape them to jars to make a fart museum. ✂

My First Fart

LAID BY: _____

DATE: _____

Post-Thanksgiving Dinner Fart

LAID BY: _____

DATE: _____

HISTORIC FARTS

Fumes
from the
Winde of Hortense Fartenberry

*Assistant Cheese Maker at
Plymouth, Massachusetts*

May 6, 1627

RARE ELECTRICALLY CHARGED FART

Created by Thomas A. Edison
1923

Four Rare Harmonic Farts

Produced by The Beatles
April 1965

43,000-Year-Old Fart
From Neanderthal Man
Preserved in Amber

MOON FART

Emitted by
Astronaut John Young
1972

The Fart Heard Around *the* World

Start of the American Revolution

Laid by Obadiah Fizzle

April 18, 1775

RARE FARTS

Cut out these labels and tape them to jars to make a fart museum. ✂

Rare Rainbow-Scented UNICORN FART

GENUINE MOSQUITO FART

Collected on August 14, 1955
Hopewell, New Jersey

World's Most TOXIC FART

EMITTED BY: _____

Caution: Do not inhale

WORLD'S LARGEST BRAIN FART

by Albert Einstein
1951

ETERNAL FART

First ripped on February 13, 1967

Still emitting sound

SAID TO BE THE FART OF

THE ELUSIVE BIGFOOT

(UNPROVEN)

UNIDENTIFIED FARTING OBJECT

Currently being studied

Start a Fartograph Collection!

Fartographs are like autographs, only they're made with gas. Have each friend fart on one of the clouds and sign it. And don't forget to add your own fart. Just think, if one of your friends ever becomes famous, you'll be the proud owner of one of their childhood farts!

This fartograph was left by:

_____
SIGNATURE

_____
DATE

This fartograph was left by:

_____
SIGNATURE

_____
DATE

This fartograph was left by:

_____
SIGNATURE

_____
DATE

This fartograph was left by:

_____
SIGNATURE

_____
DATE

Fart Trivia Game

Now that you've learned more about farts than you ever imagined, go butt-to-butt with your friends to see who scores highest in this toot trivia game.

To play, you will need:
- At least 3 players
- A timer
- Paper and pencil
- Prizes

1 **Choose a player to be the quizmaster.** The quizmaster will ask the questions and keep track of the time and how many points each team has.

2 **Separate the other players into 2 or 3 teams.** A team can be anywhere from 1 to 4 players. Decide which team goes first.

3 **Have the quizmaster ask Team 1 the first question.** Team 1 has 1½ minutes to answer it. They score 2 points if they get the right answer. If time runs out or their answer is wrong, Team 2 gets 30 seconds to answer the same question. They get 1 point if they answer correctly. Keep asking question 1 until a team answers it correctly or every team has tried and failed. Then move on to question 2.

4 **When the quizmaster has asked all the questions, add up the points.** The team with the most points wins. You can make the prize fart-related—for example, a personally delivered fresh fart from each player. Or come up with your own prize ideas.

The Questions

1 **How many times does the average person fart each day?**

    A. 10–20

    B. 20–30

    C. 40–50

    Answer: A. 10–20

2 **How long was the longest recorded fart?**

    A. 42 seconds

    B. 2 minutes and 42 seconds

    C. 10 minutes and 42 seconds

    Answer: B. 2 minutes and 42 seconds

3 **What can happen if you hold in a fart?**

    A. The fart gas goes to your toes and makes your feet stink.

    B. Your body fills with so much gas that you rise off the ground slightly.

    C. The fart may exit through your mouth in your breath.

    Answer: C. The fart may exit through your mouth in your breath.

4 **Where do people tend to fart more?**

    A. In a swimming pool

    B. At school

    C. On an airplane

    Answer: C. On an airplane

5 **Which planet smells like farts?**

    A. Mars

    B. Uranus

    C. Jupiter

    Answer: B. Uranus (It's surrounded by hydrogen sulfide, the same gas that makes farts smelly.)

> Why did the woman stop telling fart jokes?
>
> Everyone told her they stink.

6 **Which of these famous people wrote an essay about farting?**

A. Taylor Swift

B. Benjamin Franklin

C. George Washington

Answer: B. Benjamin Franklin

7 **What animal is known to make fart noises with its mouth, similar to the way people blow raspberries?**

A. Orangutan

B. Duck

C. Blowfish

Answer: A. Orangutan

8 **Which of these foods can make farts smellier?**

A. Red meat

B. Rice

C. Chocolate

Answer: A. Red meat

PFFFT!

9 **How old is the oldest known fart joke?**

A. 40 years

B. 400 years

C. 4,000 years

Answer: C. 4,000 years

10 **Which one of these fart inventions is real?**

A. A "fart thrower" that sends the sound of your fart to another person's butt

B. An alarm clock that makes fart noises and smells

C. Doggie underpants that block the smell of farts

Answer: C. Doggie underpants that block the smell of farts

11 **Which of these animals does not fart?**

A. Mouse

B. Sloth

C. Snake

Answer: B. Sloth

12 **What does *borborygmus* mean?**

A. The rumbling sound your stomach makes when there is gas inside

B. The time between when you hear a fart and when you smell it

C. A person whose farts are very boring

Answer: A. The rumbling sound your stomach makes when there is gas inside

TOOOOOT!

13 **Performer Joseph Pujol could use his farts to do what?**

A. Write his name

B. Make balloon animals

C. Blow out a candle

Answer: C. Blow out a candle

14 **What did a scientist invent so he could collect people's farts for study?**

A. Airtight pants made from Mylar

B. Hollow seat cushions

C. Boxes similar to mailboxes, only for farts

Answer: A. Airtight pants made from Mylar

***Pfft!* Hooray!** You've made it to the end of this book, which means you must have released some smelly bowel howls and doom-dusted your friends and family a few times. We hope you'll keep on farting wherever the wind takes you! Remember, not only is farting healthy, it's an essential form of human expression. Pledge to honor your right to fart freely, noisily, and odorously by signing this Declaration of Flatulence.

Declaration of Flatulence

When in the course of human digestion a small amount of gas is created and yearns to be released into the outside world, no person, institution, or government shall impede its journey. To do so not only would be unhealthy, it would deprive fellow citizens of the chance to revel in the magnificent and varied sounds and smells of human flatulence and the intense reactions these gaseous emissions provoke. In consideration of these facts, I pledge that whenever I feel the call of my intestines to bring forth a fart into the world, I shall let it rip in the name of freedom and flatulence for all.

Name: _____

Date: _____

Fart here. Pfft.

Answers

Page 10: Free the Fart!

Pages 16–17: Order Up at the Gas Station Café!

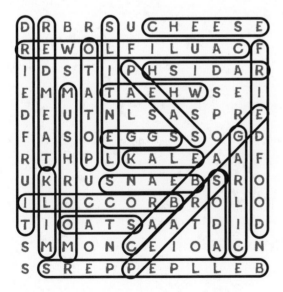

The two other fart-friendly foods hidden in the puzzle are:

Brussels sprouts and **onions**

Pages 28–29: Flatulence Is the Mother of Invention

The real inventions:

1. Fart Pills

A man named Christian Poincheval really did invent pills intended to make your farts smell like chocolate or roses. While the idea sounds appealing, it's probably not scientifically possible.

3. Doggie Underwear

These dog fart absorbers are no longer available, but the idea behind the invention is sound. The activated charcoal used to absorb odor really can remove more than 90 percent of the sulfur gases that make farts stink.

4. The Farting Car

The people at the Tesla car company have a fine sense of humor. They really did include a fart mode in their Model 3 car!

5. Flatulence in a Bottle

A company called AromaPrime makes scented oils for museums, amusement parks, and anyone who wants to make their home smell, well, unusual. One of their oils is simply called *Flatulence*. No further explanation needed.

The made-up inventions:

2. Fart Reader

6. Farting Alarm Clock

Pages 40–41: Who Farted?
Answer: Fartinand

He is the only one who fits all three clues:

1. Those who are overreacting:

Toots

Aunt Odoria

Egbert

Martin

Smellen

Fartinand

Dad

2. Those who are not accusing someone else:

Toots

Mom

Grandma Flatus

Stinky

Smellen

Fartinand

3. Those who are being accused:

Mom

Egbert

Grandma Flatus

Stinky

Uncle Pooter

Fartinand

Pages 49:
Test Your Fart Smarts

1. (B)

Eating foods (such as meat or asparagus) that contain sulfur, a chemical that smells like rotten eggs

2. True

A fart that you hold in can be reabsorbed into your bloodstream and then released through your mouth in your breath.

3. (C) Airplanes

The gas in your intestines can expand when you are at higher altitudes, such as in an airplane or at the top of a mountain. The gas needs somewhere to go, which is why you fart more.

4. True

The bacteria in the intestines continue to produce gas after a person dies, and that can lead to a few final farts.

5. (B)

They were concerned that the gases released by farts could be a fire hazard in the sealed environment of the spacecraft.

6. False

It would be nice if you could change the smell of your farts by eating sweet-smelling foods, but unfortunately, it doesn't work that way.

7. (A) Farting underwater

When you fart in the water, the gas forms a bubble that is visible.

8. False

While human farts do contain methane, which is a major contributor to global warming, the amount is tiny compared to the amount emitted by cow belches. If you want to help fight climate change, your best bet is to keep farting but eat less beef, which will mean fewer bovine burps.

Pages 51–53:
It's Time to Take the G.A.T.!
1. (B) Zebra

Zebras have a very long colon (large intestine), which means there's room for a lot of gas to build up as they digest all the plants they eat. When the gas finally blasts forth, you can hear it trumpet across the eastern plains of Africa. Even better is the show the zebra puts on when it gets startled and runs. The motion pushes gas out of its butt and it farts with every step, like a galloping drum machine.

2. (A) Bird

Birds lack the gas-producing bacteria in their gut that are necessary to fart. So while you may see a bird soar on the wind, you'll never see one break wind. There is one bird, though, that *sounds* like it's farting when it takes flight: the partridge. But don't be fooled. The sound comes from the bird's wings, which make a whirring noise similar to a fart. In fact, the word *partridge* is thought to come from the Greek word for "breaking wind."

3. True

Goats produce a lot of gas because, like cows, they have four stomachs. In 2015, more than 2,000 goats were being moved from Australia to Malaysia on an airplane. They produced so much gas that the fire alarm went off and the pilot had to make an emergency landing.

4. (A) Seal and sea lion

Seals and sea lions eat huge amounts of fish, which is a proven recipe for putrid farts. One zoologist compared seal farts to "rotten fish mixed with rotten eggs," and zookeepers report that the sea lion's farts are equally wretched.

5. (B) Frighten predators

When threatened, this rare, highly venomous snake contracts the muscles in its cloaca—the hole from which it pees and poops—which forces out the air inside and makes a popping sound much like a human fart. The noise startles predators and warns them to get lost—good advice considering how deadly this snake is.

6. (C) Millipede

The many-legged millipede has everything it takes to fart: a gut that produces gas and an opening in the back for the gas to exit. You won't ever hear it toot, though. At the point where the gas exits, the millipede has a valve that scientists think may silence its farts. If only we all could be so lucky.

7. True

One species of an insect called the beaded lacewing lays its eggs next to a termite nest. When the larvae hatch, they enter the nest and fart on the termites. A chemical in the farts paralyzes the termites long enough for the larvae to eat them. The fart has no warning sound or smell, but it's a clear case of murder by flatulence.

8. (B) Termite

This little insect gets the award for tiny but mighty when it comes to farting out methane. Termites produce an impressive 1 to 3 percent of all methane emissions. That might not sound like a lot, but it's a big achievement when you consider how tiny a termite toot is. Termites produce a lot of methane for two reasons: Their diet of wood and leaves makes them gassy, and there are a lot of termites on the planet (a single colony may contain several million insects). They've been at it for a long time, too: Some ancient termites preserved in fossils have tiny fart bubbles coming out of their rear ends.

9. (A) Communicate with other herring

Herring often gather in groups at night for protection from predators. They can't see well in the dark, though, so they need another way to find each other. That's where farts come in. Some species of herring expel air through their butts, producing a high-pitched fart that other herring recognize. The farts are like a secret code—the sound is too high for predators to hear.

10. (B) It comes out with their breath.

Sloths eat nothing but leaves, and digesting all that plant matter gives them major gas. But instead of getting rid of it by farting, sloths absorb the gas into their bloodstream and then breathe it out—which is one good reason you should avoid kissing a sloth.

Pages 54-55:
Butt Burps and Cheek Squeaks

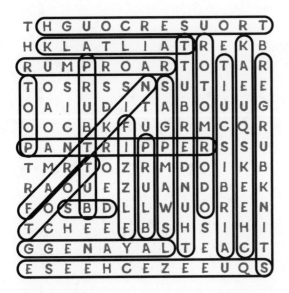

The joke:

Why did the worker in the sandwich shop fart so much?

Answer: THE BOSS SAID TO CUT MORE CHEESE.

Pages 60-61:
Find the Beastly Farters

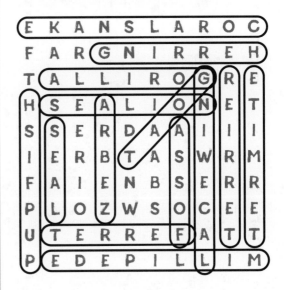

The answer to the joke is:

They FARTED RAINBOWS.

What did the big fart say to the little fart?

Everything I know I learned in kinderfarten.

Fart here

Fart here

Fart here

Fart here

Fart here

Fart here

About The Author

Julie Winterbottom is the author of *Pranklopedia* and *Frightlopedia* and the former editor-in-chief of *Nickelodeon Magazine*, where she discovered the true meaning of farts. She lives in Beacon, New York.

About The Illustrator

Clau Souza is an illustrator of a variety of fun projects for kids. She believes that this is a great excuse to keep in touch with her inner child. She used to fart in Brazil— where she lived most of her life, but now she's farting in Toronto, Canada.